# HOLINESS BEFITS YOUR HOUSE

## Canonization of Edith Stein
## — A Documentation —

*Edited by John Sullivan, OCD STD*

ICS Publications
Institute of Carmelite Studies
Washington, DC
2000

Thanks to the Tipografia Vaticana, *L'Osservatore Romano* and America Press
for reprinted materials.

ICS Publications
2131 Lincoln Road NE
Washington, DC 20002-1199
800 - 832-8489

*Typeset by Stephen Tiano Graphic Design/Editing Services*
*Cover design by Nancy Gurganus of Grey Coat Graphics*
*Cover woodcut by Robert F. McGovern*

**Library of Congress Cataloging-in-Publications Data**

Holiness befits your house: canonization of Edith Stein: a documentation/
edited by John Sullivan.
    p.   cm.
Includes bibliographical references.
ISBN 0-935216-72-3
    1. Stein, Edith, 1891-1942. I. Sullivan, John, 1942-

BX4700.S74 H65 1999
282'.092-dc21
  [B]
                                         99-049939

# Contents

# Editor's Preface

The last Discalced Carmelite to be canonized a saint in the twentieth century claimed many "houses" as her own: Edith Stein now belongs to the Eternal House of God as one of his holy ones who suffered through the troubled times of mid-century Europe yet remained faithful to God's voice heard in its several tonalities throughout her life. In following God's lead and guidance she called Judaism her home in her early years; then she chose Catholicism as her second religious allegiance; finally she entered Saint Teresa's dwelling places to lead an existence of intense prayer during the last decade of her days on earth.

This compilation does not attempt to fill in detail the broad canvas of her fascinating life, nor capture the full stir of lively debate unleashed by an upsurge in attention to her—use of the select bibliography at the end will acquaint the reader further. Instead, our goal is to provide significant official statements alongside others made by keenly interested observers of Saint Edith or Teresa Benedicta's ongoing influence on interreligious dialogue in our country.

Timeframe for the selections is primarily the canonization itself which occurred on Sunday, October 11, 1998. Our religious order sponsored a commemoration/thanksgiving afterwards on March 14, 1999, Laetare Sunday, located in the nation's capital: the second group of texts except one derive from that event. Because we at ICS Publications receive requests for the beatification homily that we published in *Carmelite Studies* 4 (now out of print), it seemed worthwhile including it in this set of texts, many of which originated in a liturgical context. Given her ever keen interest in good worship Saint Edith would gladly have assented to a collection like this designed to honor her and the many words of inspiration she left behind. May they prove helpful to all who read them and wish to deepen their knowledge of her.

John Sullivan, OCD
Memorial of Saint Edith
August 9, 1999

# *PAPAL STATEMENTS*

# Homily at Canonization Eucharist
## Pope John Paul II

*"For the honor of the Blessed Trinity, the exaltation of the Catholic faith and the fostering of the Christian life, by the authority of our Lord Jesus Christ, of the holy Apostles Peter and Paul, and our own, after due deliberation and frequent prayers for the divine assistance, and having sought the counsel of our Brother Bishops, we declare and define that Bl. Teresa Benedicta of the Cross, Edith Stein, is a saint and we enroll her among the saints, decreeing that she is to be venerated in the whole Church as one of the saints. In the name of the Father, and of the Son and of the Holy Spirit."*

With these solemn words pronounced in Latin on Sunday, October 11, Pope John Paul II canonized St. Teresa Benedicta of the Cross, Edith Stein, a Jewish philosopher, convert to the Catholic faith, Carmelite nun and martyr at Auschwitz. The canonization took place during a solemn concelebrated Mass in St. Peter's Square. After the gospel text (Jn 4:19-24) was chanted in Latin and Greek, the Holy Father gave the following homily in Italian and German:

1. "Far be it from me to glory except in the cross of our Lord Jesus Christ' (Gal 6: 14). St. Paul's words to the Galatians, which we have just heard, are well suited to the human and spiritual experience of Teresa Benedicta of the Cross, who has been solemnly enrolled among the saints today. She too can repeat with the Apostle: "Far be it from me to glory except in the cross of our Lord Jesus Christ."

The cross of Christ! Ever blossoming, the tree of the cross continues to bear new fruits of salvation. This is why believers look with confidence to the cross, drawing from its mystery of love the courage and strength to walk faithfully in the footsteps of the crucified and risen Christ. Thus the message of the cross has entered the hearts of so many men and women and changed their lives.

The spiritual experience of Edith Stein is an eloquent example of this extraordinary interior renewal. A young woman in search of the truth has become a saint and martyr through the silent workings

of divine grace: Teresa Benedicta of the Cross, who from heaven re-
peats to us today all the words that marked her life: "Far be it from
me to glory except in the cross of our Lord Jesus Christ."

2. On May 1, 1987, during my pastoral visit to Germany, I had
the joy of beatifying this generous witness to the faith in the city of
Cologne. Today, 11 years later, here in Rome, in St. Peter's Square,
I am able solemnly to present this eminent daughter of Israel and
faithful daughter of the church as a saint to the whole world.

Today, as then, we bow to the memory of Edith Stein, proclaiming the indomitable witness she bore during her life and especially
by her death. Now alongside Teresa of Avila and Thérèse of Lisieux,
another Teresa takes her place among the host of saints who do
honor to the Carmelite Order.

Dear brothers and sisters who have gathered for this solemn
celebration, let us give glory to God for what he has accomplished
in Edith Stein.

### We remember all concentration camp victims with respect

3. I greet the many pilgrims who have come to Rome, particularly the members of the Stein family who have wanted to be with us
on this joyful occasion. I also extend a cordial greeting to the rep-
resentatives of the Carmelite community, which became a "second
family" for Teresa Benedicta of the Cross.

I also welcome the official delegation from the Federal Republic
of Germany, led by Helmut Kohl, the outgoing Federal Chancellor,
whom I greet with heartfelt respect. Moreover, I greet the representa-
tives of the states of North Rhine-Westphalia and Rhineland-Palatinate
and the Mayor of Cologne.

An official delegation has also come from my country, led by
Prime Minister Jerzy Buzek. I extend a cordial greeting to them.

I would particularly like to mention the pilgrims from the Dio-
ceses of Wroclaw (Breslau), Cologne, Münster, Speyer, Kraków and
Bielsko-Zywiec who have come with their Cardinals, Bishops and
pastors. They join the numerous groups of the faithful from Germany,
the United States of America and my homeland, Poland.

4. Dear brothers and sisters! Because she was Jewish, Edith Stein
was taken with her sister Rosa and many other Catholic Jews from
the Netherlands to the concentration camp in Auschwitz, where she

died with them in the gas chambers. Today we remember them all with deep respect. A few days before her deportation, the woman religious had dismissed the question about a possible rescue: "Do not do it! Why should I be spared? Is it not right that I should gain no advantage from my baptism? If I cannot share the lot of my brothers and sisters, my life, in a certain sense, is destroyed."

From now on, as we celebrate the memory of this new saint from year to year, we must also remember the Shoah, that cruel plan to exterminate a people, a plan to which millions of our Jewish brothers and sisters fell victim. May the Lord let his face shine upon them and grant them peace (cf. Nm 6:25f).

For the love of God and man, once again I raise an anguished cry: May such criminal deeds never be repeated against any ethnic group, against any race, in any corner of this world! It is a cry to everyone: to all people of goodwill; to all who believe in the Just and Eternal God; to all who know they are joined to Christ, the Word of God made man. We must all stand together: human dignity is at stake. There is only one human family. The new saint also insisted on this: "Our love of neighbor is the measure of our love of God. For Christians and not only for them no one is a 'stranger.' The love of Christ knows no borders."

*Only the love of Christ makes us truly free*

5. Dear brothers and sisters! The love of Christ was the fire that inflamed the life of St. Teresa Benedicta of the Cross. Long before she realized it, she was caught by this fire. At the beginning she devoted herself to freedom. For a long time Edith Stein was a seeker. Her mind never tired of searching and her heart always yearned for hope. She traveled the arduous path of philosophy with passionate enthusiasm. Eventually she was rewarded: she seized the truth. Or better: she was seized by it. Then she discovered that truth had a name: Jesus Christ. From that moment on, the incarnate Word was her One and All. Looking back as a Carmelite on this period of her life, she wrote to a Benedictine nun: "Whoever seeks the truth is seeking God, whether consciously or unconsciously."

Although Edith Stein had been brought up religiously by her Jewish mother, at the age of 14 she consciously and deliberately stopped praying." She wanted to rely exclusively on herself and was concerned to assert her freedom in making decisions about her life. At the end of a long journey, she came to the surprising realization: only those who commit themselves to the love of Christ become truly free.

This woman had to face the challenges of such a radically changing century as our own. Her experience is an example to us. The modern world boasts of the enticing door which says: everything is permitted. It ignores the narrow gate of discernment and renunciation. I am speaking especially to you, young Christians, particularly to the many altar servers who have come to Rome these days on pilgrimage: Pay attention! Your life is not an endless series of open doors! Listen to your heart! Do not stay on the surface, but go to the heart of things! And when the time is right, have the courage to decide! The Lord is waiting for you to put your freedom in his good hands.

6. St. Teresa Benedicta of the Cross was able to understand that the love of Christ and human freedom are intertwined, because love and truth have an intrinsic relationship. The quest for truth and its expression in love did not seem at odds to her; on the contrary she realized that they call for one another.

In our time, truth is often mistaken for the opinion of the majority. In addition, there is a widespread belief that one should use the truth even against love or vice versa. But truth and love need each other. St. Teresa Benedicta is a witness to this. The "martyr for love," who gave her life for her friends; let no one surpass her in love. At the same time, with her whole being she sought the truth, of which she wrote: "No spiritual work comes into the world without great suffering. It always challenges the whole person."

St. Teresa Benedicta of the Cross says to us all: Do not accept anything as the truth if it lacks love. And do not accept anything as love which lacks truth! One without the other becomes a destructive lie.

*Mystery of the Cross gradually enveloped her whole life*

7. Finally, the new saint teaches us that love for Christ undergoes suffering. Whoever truly loves does not stop at the prospect of suffering: he accepts communion in suffering with the one he loves.

Aware of what her Jewish origins implied, Edith Stein spoke eloquently about them: "Beneath the cross I understood the destiny of God's People. . .Indeed, today I know far better what it means to be the Lord's bride under the sign of the cross. But since it is a mystery, it can never be understood by reason alone."

The mystery of the cross gradually enveloped her whole life, spurring her to the point of making the supreme sacrifice. As a bride on the cross, Sr. Teresa Benedicta did not only write profound pages about the "science of the cross," but was thoroughly trained in the school of the cross. Many of our contemporaries would like to silence the cross. But nothing is more eloquent than the cross when silenced! The true message of suffering is a lesson of love. Love makes suffering fruitful and suffering deepens love.

Through the experience of the cross, Edith Stein was able to open the way to a new encounter with the God of Abraham, Isaac and Jacob, the Father of our Lord Jesus Christ. Faith and the cross proved inseparable to her. Having matured in the school of the cross, she found the roots to which the tree of her own life was attached. She understood that it was very important for her "to be a daughter of the chosen people and to belong to Christ not only spiritually, but also through blood."

8. "God is spirit, and those who worship him must worship in spirit and truth" (Jn 4: 24). Dear brothers and sisters, the divine Teacher spoke these words to the Samaritan woman at Jacob's well. What he gave his chance but attentive listener we also find in the life of Edith Stein, in her "ascent of Mount Carmel." The depth of the divine mystery became perceptible to her in the silence of contemplation. Gradually, throughout her life, as she grew in the knowledge of God, worshipping him in spirit and truth, she experienced ever more clearly her specific vocation to ascend the cross with Christ, to embrace it with serenity and trust, to love it by following in the footsteps of her beloved Spouse: St. Teresa Benedicta of the Cross is offered to us today as a model to inspire us and a protectress to call upon.

We give thanks to God for this gift. May the new saint be an example to us in our commitment to serve freedom, in our search for the truth. My her witness constantly strengthen the bridge of mutual understanding between Jews and Christians. St. Teresa Benedicta of the Cross, pray for us! Amen.

Source: *L'Osservatore Romano*, Weekly Edition in English, no. 41, October 14, 1998, 1 & 10.

# Biography in Canonization Eucharist Booklet
## Pontifical Office of Ceremonies

*To all who attend the canonization eucharist a celebration booklet is distributed. In it are the Mass prayers, the formula of canonization, scripture readings, and chants. At the beginning is a concise account of the life of the new saint in six languages. The following curriculum vitae appeared in the booklet for Edith Stein's canonization:*

"We bow down before the testimony of the life and death of Edith Stein, an outstanding daughter of' Israel and at the same time a daughter of the Carmelite Order, Sister Teresa Benedicta of the Cross, a personality who united within her rich life a dramatic synthesis of our century. It was the synthesis of a history full of deep wounds that are still hurting. . .and also the synthesis of the full truth about man. All this came together in a single heart that remained restless and unfulfilled until it finally found rest in God." These were the words of Pope John Paul II when he beatified Edith Stein in Cologne on May 1, 1987.

*Who was this woman?*

Edith Stein was born in Breslau on October 12, 1891, the youngest of 11, as her family were celebrating Yom Kippur, that most important Jewish festival, the Feast of Atonement. "More than anything else, this helped make the youngest child very precious to her mother." Being born on this day was like a foreshadowing to Edith, a future Carmelite nun.

Edith's father, who ran a timber business, died when she had only just turned [=approached] two. Her mother, a very devout, hard-working, strong-willed and truly wonderful woman, now had to fend for herself and to look after the family and their large business. However, she did not succeed in keeping up a living faith in her children. Edith lost her faith in God. "I consciously decided, of my own volition, to give up praying," she said.

In 1911 she passed her school-leaving exam with flying colors and enrolled at the University of Breslau to study German history, though this was a mere "bread-and-butter" choice. Her real interest was in philosophy and in women's issues. She became a member of the Prussian Society for Women's Franchise. "When I was at school and during my first years at university," she wrote later, "I was a radical suffragette. Then I lost interest in the whole issue. Now I am looking for purely pragmatic solutions."

In 1913, Edith Stein transferred to Göttingen University, to study under the mentorship of Edmund Husserl. She became his pupil and teaching assistant, and he later tutored her for a doctorate. At the time, anyone who was interested in philosophy was fascinated by Husserl's new view of reality, whereby the world as we perceive it does not merely exist in a Kantian way, in our subjective perception. His pupils saw his philosophy as a return to objects: "back to things." Husserl's phenomenology unwittingly led many of his pupils to the Christian faith. In Göttingen Edith Stein also met the philosopher Max Scheler, who directed her attention to Roman Catholicism. Nevertheless, she did not neglect her "bread-and-butter" studies and passed her degree with distinction in January 1915, though she did not follow it up with teacher training.

"I no longer have a life of my own," she wrote at the beginning of the First World War, having done a nursing course and gone to serve in an Austrian field hospital. This was a hard time for her, during which she looked after the sick in the typhus ward, worked in an operating theater, and saw young people die. When the hospital was dissolved, in 1916, she followed Husserl as his assistant to the German city of Freiburg, where she passed her doctorate *summa cum laude* (with the utmost distinction) in 1917, after writing a thesis on "The Problem of Empathy."

During this period she went to Frankfurt Cathedral and saw a woman with a shopping basket going in to kneel for a brief prayer. "This was something totally new to me. In the synagogues and Protestant churches I had visited people simply went to the services. Here, however, I saw someone coming straight from the busy marketplace into this empty church, as if she was going to have an intimate conversation. It was something I never forgot." Toward the end of her dissertation she wrote: "There have been people who believed that a sudden change had occurred within them and that this was a result of God's grace." How could she come to such a conclusion?

Edith Stein had been good friends with Husserl's Göttingen assistant, Adolf Reinach, and his wife. When Reinach fell in Flanders in November 1917, Edith went to Göttingen to visit his widow. The Reinachs had converted to Protestantism. Edith felt uneasy about meeting the young widow at first, but was surprised when she actually met with a woman of faith." This was my first encounter with the cross and the divine power it imparts to those who bear it. . .it was the moment when my unbelief collapsed and Christ began to shine his light on me—Christ in the mystery of the cross." Later, she wrote: "Things were in God's plan which I had not planned at all. I am coming to the living faith and conviction that–from God's point of view–there is no chance and that the whole of my life, down to every detail, has been mapped out in God's divine providence and makes complete and perfect sense in God's all-seeing eyes."

In Autumn 1918 Edith Stein gave up her job as Husserl's teaching assistant. She wanted to work independently. It was not until 1930 that she saw Husserl again after her conversion, and she shared with him about her faith, as she would have liked him to become a Christian, too. [Ed. note: in fact Husserl was baptized a Lutheran in Vienna shortly before his marriage in 1887.] Then she wrote down the amazing words: "Every time I feel my powerlessness and inability to influence people directly, I become more keenly aware of the necessity of my own holocaust[um]." Edith Stein wanted to obtain a professorship, a goal that was impossible for a woman at the time. Husserl wrote the following reference: "Should academic careers be opened up to ladies, then I can recommend her wholeheartedly and as my first choice for admission to a professorship." Later, she was refused a professorship on account of her Jewishness.

Back in Breslau, Edith Stein began to write articles about the philosophical foundation of psychology. However, she also read the New Testament, Kierkegaard and Ignatius of Loyola's Spiritual Exercises. She felt that one could not just read a book like that, but had to put it into practice.

In the summer of 1921 she spent several weeks in Bergzabern (in the Palatinate) on the country estate of Hedwig Conrad-Martius, another pupil of Husserl's. Hedwig had converted to Protestantism with her husband. One evening Edith picked up an [sic] autobiography of St. Teresa of Avila and read this book all night. "When I had finished the book, I said to myself: This is the truth." Later, looking back on her life, she wrote: "My longing for truth was a single prayer."

On January 1, 1922 Edith Stein was baptized. It was the Feast of the Circumcision of Jesus, when Jesus entered into the covenant of Abraham. Edith Stein stood by the baptismal font, wearing Hedwig Conrad-Martius' white wedding cloak. Hedwig was her godmother. "I had given up practicing my Jewish religion when I was a 14-year-old girl and did not begin to feel Jewish again until I had returned to God." From this moment on she was continually aware that she belonged to Christ not only spiritually, but also through her blood. At the Feast of the Purification of Mary–another day with an Old Testament reference–she was confirmed by the Bishop of Speyer in his private chapel.

After her conversion she went straight to Breslau: "Mother," she said, "I am a Catholic." The two women cried. Hedwig Conrad-Martius wrote: "Behold, two Israelites indeed, in whom there is no deceit!" (cf. John 1:47)

Immediately after her conversion she wanted to join a Carmelite convent. However, her spiritual mentors, Vicar-General Schwind of Speyer, and Erich Przywara SJ, stopped her from doing so. Until Easter 1931 she held a position teaching German and history at the Dominican Sisters' school and teacher training college of St. Magdalen's Convent in Speyer. At the same time she was encouraged by Arch-Abbot Raphael Walzer of Beuron Abbey to accept extensive speaking engagements, mainly on women's issues. "During, the time immediately before and quite some time after my conversion I thought that leading a religious life meant giving up all earthly things and having one's mind fixed on divine things only. Gradually, however, I learned that other things are expected of us in this world. . .I even believe that the deeper someone is drawn to God, the more he has to 'get beyond himself' in this sense, that is, go into the world and carry divine life into it." She worked enormously hard, translating the letters and diaries of Cardinal Newman from his pre-Catholic period as well as Thomas Aquinas's *Quaestiones Disputatae de Veritate.* The latter was a very free translation, for the sake of dialogue with modern philosophy. Erich Przywara also encouraged her to write her own philosophical works. She learned that it was possible to "pursue scholarship as a service to God. . .It was not until I had understood this that I seriously began to approach academic work again." To gain strength for her life and work, she frequently went to the Benedictine Monastery of Beuron, to celebrate the great festivals of the church year.

In 1931 Edith Stein left the convent school in Speyer and devoted herself to working for a professorship again, this time in Breslau and Freiburg, though her endeavors were in vain. It was then that she wrote *Potency and Act*, a study of the central concepts developed by Thomas Aquinas. Later, at the Carmelite Convent in Cologne, she re-wrote this study to produce her main philosophical and theological oeuvre, *Finite and Eternal Being*. By then, however, it was no longer possible to print the book.

In 1932 she accepted a lectureship position at the Roman Catholic division of the German Institute for Educational Studies at the University of Münster, where she developed her anthropology. She successfully combined scholarship and faith in her work and her teaching, seeking to be a "tool of the Lord" in everything she taught. "If anyone comes to me, I want to lead them to him."

In 1933 darkness broke out over Germany. "I had heard of severe measures against Jews before. But now it dawned on me that God had laid his hand heavily on his people, and that the destiny of these people would also be mine." The Aryan Law of the Nazis made it impossible for Edith Stein to continue teaching. "If I can't go on here, then there are no longer any opportunities for me in Germany," she wrote, "I had become a stranger in the world."

The Arch-Abbot of Beuron, Walzer, now no longer stopped her from entering a Carmelite convent. While in Speyer, she had already taken a vow of poverty, chastity and obedience. In 1933 she met with the prioress of the Carmelite Convent in Cologne. "Human activities cannot help us, but only the suffering of Christ. It is my desire to share in it."

Edith Stein went to Breslau for the last time, to say good-bye to her mother and her family. Her last day at home was her birthday, October 12, which was also the last day of the Feast of Tabernacles. Edith went to the synagogue with her mother. It was a hard day for the two women. "Why did you get to know it [Christianity]?" her mother asked, "I don't want to say anything against him. He may have been a very good person. But why did he make himself God?"

Edith's mother cried. The following day Edith was on the train to Cologne. "I did not feel any passionate joy. What I had just experienced was too terrible. But I felt a profound peace—in the safe haven of God's will." From now on she wrote to her mother every week, though she never received any replies. Instead, her sister Rosa sent her news from Breslau.

Edith joined the Carmelite Convent of Cologne on October 14, and her investiture took place on April 15, 1934. The mass was celebrated by the Arch-Abbot of Beuron. Edith Stein was now known as Sister Teresia Benedicta a Cruce—Teresa, Blessed of the Cross. In 1938 she wrote: "I understood the cross as the destiny of God's people, which was beginning to be apparent at the time (1933). 1 felt that those who understood the cross of Christ should take it upon themselves on everybody's behalf. Of course, I know better now what it means to be wedded to the Lord in the sign of the cross. However, one can never comprehend it, because it is a mystery." On April 21, 1935 she took her temporary vows. On September 14, 1936, the renewal of her vows coincided with her mother's death in Breslau. "My mother held on to her faith to the last moment. But as her faith and her firm trust in her God. . .were the last thing that was still alive in the throes of her death, I am confident that she will have met a very merciful judge and that she is now my most faithful helper, so that I can reach the goal as well."

When she made her eternal [=perpetual] profession on April 21, 1938, she had the words of St. John of the Cross printed on her devotional picture: "Henceforth my only vocation is to love." Her final work was to be devoted to this author.

Edith Stein's entry into the Carmelite Order was not escapism. "Those who join the Carmelite Order are not lost to their near and dear ones, but have been won for them, because it is our vocation to intercede to God for everyone." In particular, she interceded to God for her people: "I keep thinking of Queen Esther who was taken away from her people precisely because God wanted her to plead with the king on behalf of her nation. I am a very poor and powerless little Esther, but the King who has chosen me is infinitely great and merciful. This is great comfort." (October 31, 1938)

On November 9, 1938 the anti-Semitism of the Nazis became apparent to the whole world. Synagogues were burnt, and the Jewish people were subjected to terror. The prioress of the Carmelite

Convent in Cologne did her utmost to take Sister Teresa Benedicta of the Cross abroad. On New Year's Eve 1938 she was smuggled across the border into the Netherlands, to the Carmelite Convent in Echt in the Province of Limburg. This is where she wrote her will [and testament] on June 9, 1939: "Even now I accept the death that God has prepared for me in complete submission and with joy as being his most holy will for me. I ask the Lord to accept my life and my death. . .so that the Lord will be accepted by his people and that his Kingdom may come in glory, for the salvation of Germany and the peace of the world."

While in the Cologne convent, Edith Stein had been given permission to start her academic studies again. Among other things, she wrote about "Life in a Jewish Family" (that is, her own family): "I simply want to report what I experienced as part of Jewish humanity," she said, pointing out that "we who grew up in Judaism have a duty to bear witness. . .to the young generation who are brought up in racial hatred from early childhood."

In Echt, Edith Stein hurriedly completed her study of "The Church's Teacher of Mysticism and the Father of the Carmelites, John of the Cross, on the Occasion of the 400th Anniversary of His Birth, 1542-1942." In 1941 she wrote to a friend, who was also a member of her order: "One can only gain a *scientia crucis* (knowledge of the cross) if one has thoroughly experienced the cross. I have been convinced of this from the first moment onwards and have said with all my heart: 'Ave Crux, Spes unica' (I welcome you, cross, our only hope)." Her study on St. John of the Cross is entitled: "Science of the Cross" (*Kreuzeswissenschaft*).

Edith Stein was arrested by the Gestapo on August 2, 1942, while she was in the chapel with the other sisters. She was to report within five minutes, together with her sister Rosa, who had also converted and was serving at the Echt convent. Her last words to be heard in Echt were addressed to Rosa: "Come, we are going for our people."

Together with many other Jewish Christians, the two women were taken to a transit camp in Amersfoort and then to Westerbork. This was an act of retaliation against the letter of protest written by the Dutch Roman Catholic bishops against the pogroms and deportations of Jews. Edith commented, "I never knew that people could be like this, neither did I know that my brothers and sisters would have to suffer like this. . .I pray for them every hour. Will God hear my prayers? He will certainly hear them in their distress." Prof. Jan Nota, who was greatly attached to her, wrote later: "She is a witness to God's presence in a world where God is absent."

On August 7, early in the morning, 987 Jews were deported to Auschwitz. It was probably on August 9 that Sister Teresa Benedicta of the Cross, her sister and many other of her people were gassed.

When Edith Stein was beatified in Cologne on May 1, 1987, the Church honored "a daughter of Israel," as Pope John Paul II put it, "who, as a Catholic during Nazi persecution, remained faithful to the crucified Lord Jesus Christ and, as a Jew, to her people in loving faithfulness."

Source: Booklet *Cappella Papale presieduta dal Santo Padre Giovanni Paolo II per la canonizzazione della Beata Teresa Benedetta della Croce, Edith Stein, Monaca Professa Carmelitana Scalza, Martire. Piazza S. Pietro, 11 Ottobre 1998, XXVIII Domenica "Per Annum"* (Vatican City: Tipografia Vaticana, 1998), pp. 25-32.

# Edith Stein in the Encyclical "Fides et Ratio"
## Pope John Paul II

*Within one week of canonizing Sr Teresa Benedicta of the Cross at St. Peter's Pope John Paul II issued an encyclical letter about the relationship between reason and faith in which he recommends the study of Edith Stein's writings along with other important believer philosophers. As the following text attests, she is the only woman philosopher mentioned alongside the modern thinkers valued by Papa Wojtyla.*

no. 74

. . .The fruitfulness of this relationship [between philosophy and the Word of God] is confirmed by the experience of great Christian theologians who also distinguished themselves as great philosophers, bequeathing to us writings of such high speculative value as to warrant comparison with the masters of ancient philosophy. . . We see the same fruitful relationship between philosophy and the Word of God in the courageous research pursued by more recent thinkers, among whom I gladly mention, in a Western context, figures such as John Henry Newman, Antonio Rosmini, Jacques Maritain, Etienne Gilson and Edith Stein, in an Eastern context, eminent scholars such as Vladimir S. Soloviev, Pavel A. Florensky, Petr Chaadaev and Vladimir N. Lossky. . . .

Source: *L'Osservatore Romano,* Weekly Edition in English, no. 41, October 14, 1998, insert p. XI. (Same issue that carries the Pope's homily for the canonization ceremony at St. Peter's.)

# Homily at Beatification Eucharist
## Pope John Paul II

*During his second pastoral visit to Germany Pope John Paul II visited Cologne, the city where Edith Stein entered religious life. While there he went to the Müngersdorfer outdoor stadium on Friday May 1, 1987 and began ceremonies at 10:00am that beatified Sr. Teresa Benedicta of the Cross. His words after the gospel were the following:*

"These are the ones who have survived the time of great distress; they have washed their robes and made them white in the blood of the Lamb" (Rv 7:14).

1. Today we greet in profound honor and holy joy a daughter of the Jewish people, rich in wisdom and courage, among these blessed men and women. Having grown up in the strict traditions of Israel, and having lived a life of virtue and self-denial in a religious order, she demonstrated her heroic character on the way to the extermination camp. Unified with our crucified Lord, she gave her life "for genuine peace" and "for the people" (see *Edith Stein, Judin, Philosophin, Ordensfrau, Martyrin*).

Cardinal, dear brothers and sisters:

Today's beatification marks the realization of a long-outstanding wish on the part of the Archdiocese of Cologne as well as on the part of many individuals and groups within the church. Seven years ago the members of the German bishops' conference sent a unanimous request for this beatification to the Holy See. Numerous bishops from other countries joined them in making this request. As such, we are all greatly gratified that I am able to fulfill this wish today and can present Sister Teresa Benedicta of the Cross to the faithful on behalf of the church as blessed in the glory of God. From this moment on we can honor her as a martyr and ask for her intercession at the throne of God. In this I would like to express congratulations to all, most of all to her fellow sisters in the order of Our Lady of Mount Carmel here in Cologne and in Echt as well as in the entire order. The fact that Jewish brothers and sisters, relatives of Edith Stein's in particular, are present at this liturgical ceremony today fills us with great joy and gratitude.

### A Call for Help

2. "O Lord, manifest yourself in the time of our distress and give us courage" (Est 4:17).

The words of this call for help from the first reading of today's liturgy were spoken by Esther, a daughter of Israel, at the time of the Babylonian captivity. Her prayer, which she directs to the Lord God at a time when her people were exposed to a deadly threat, are profoundly moving.

"My Lord, our king, you alone are God. Help me, who am alone and have no help but you, for I am taking my life in my hand. . . You, O Lord, chose Israel from among all peoples. . .and our fathers from among all their ancestors as a lasting heritage. . .be mindful of us, O Lord. . .Save us by your power" (Est 4:17).

Esther's deathly fear arose when, under the influence of the mighty Haman, an archenemy of the Jews, the order for their destruction was given out in all of the Persian empire. With God's help and by sacrificing her own life Esther rendered a key contribution toward saving her people.

3. Today's liturgy places this more than 2,000-year-old prayer for help in the mouth of Edith Stein, a servant of God and a daughter of Israel in our century. This prayer became relevant again when here, in the heart of Europe, a new plan for the destruction of the Jews was laid out. An insane ideology decided on this plan in the name of a wretched form of racism and carried it out mercilessly.

Extermination camps and crematoriums were rapidly built, parallel to the dramatic events of World War II. Several million sons and daughters of Israel were killed at these places of horror–from children to the elderly. The enormously powerful machinery of the totalitarian state spared no one and undertook extremely cruel measures against those who had the courage to defend the Jews.

4. Edith Stein died at the Auschwitz extermination camp, the daughter of a martyred people. Despite the fact that she moved from

Cologne to the Dutch Carmelite community in Echt, her protection against the growing persecution of the Jews was only temporary. The Nazi policy of exterminating the Jews was rapidly implemented in Holland, too, after the country had been occupied. Jews who had converted to Christianity were initially left alone. However, when the Catholic bishops in the Netherlands issued a pastoral letter in which they sharply protested against the deportation of the Jews, the Nazi rulers reacted by ordering the extermination of Catholic Jews as well. This was the cause of the martyrdom suffered by Sister Teresa Benedicta of the Cross together with her sister Rosa, who had also sought refuge with the Carmelites in Echt.

On leaving their convent Edith took her sister by the hand and said: "Come, we will go for our people." On the strength of Christ's willingness to sacrifice himself for others she saw in her seeming impotence a way to render a final service to her people. A few years previously she had compared herself with Queen Esther in exile at the Persian court. In one of her letters we read: "I am confident that the Lord has taken my life for all (Jews). I always have to think of Queen Esther, who was taken away from her people for the express purpose of standing before the king for her people. I am the very poor, weak and small Esther, but the king who selected me is infinitely great and merciful."

*Incessant Search for Truth*

5. Dear brothers and sisters, the second reading in this special Mass is from St. Paul's letter to the Galatians. He wrote there: "May I never boast of anything but the cross of our Lord, Jesus Christ. Through it, the world has been crucified to me and I to the world" (Gal 6:14).

During her lifetime, Edith Stein too encountered the secret of the cross that St. Paul announces to the Christians in this letter. Edith encountered Christ and this encounter led her step by step into the Carmelite community. In the extermination camp she died as a daughter of Israel "for the glory of the Most Holy Name" and, at the same time, as Sister Teresa Benedicta of the Cross, literally, "blessed by the cross."

Edith Stein's entire life is characterized by an incessant search for truth and is illuminated by the blessing of the cross of Christ. She encountered the cross for the first time in the strongly religious widow of a university friend. Instead of despairing, this woman took strength and hope from the cross of Christ. Later she wrote about this: "It was my first encounter with the cross and the divine strength it gives those who bear it. . .It was the moment in which my atheism collapsed. . . and Christ shone brightly: Christ in the mystery of the cross."

Her own life and the cross she had to bear were intimately connected with the destiny of the Jewish people, In a prayer she confessed to the Savior that she knew that it was his cross that was now being laid on the Jewish people and that those who realized this would have to accept it willingly on behalf of all the others. "I wanted to do it–all he has to do is show me how." At the same time she attains the inner certainty that God has heard her prayer. The more often swastikas were seen on the streets, the higher the cross of Jesus Christ rose up in her life. When she entered the Carmelite order of nuns in Cologne as Sister Teresia Benedicta a Cruce in order to experience the cross of Christ even more profoundly, she knew that she was "married to the Lord in the sign of the cross." On the day of her first vows she felt, in her own words, "like the bride of the lamb." She was convinced that her heavenly groom would introduce her to the profound mysteries of the cross.

### Ethical Idealism

6. Teresa Blessed by the Cross was the name given in a religious order to a woman who began her spiritual life with the conviction that God does not exist. At that time, in her school girl years and when she was at university, her life was not yet filled with the redeeming cross of Christ. However, it was already object of constant searching on the part of her sharp intellect. As a 15-year-old schoolgirl in her hometown of Breslau [Ed. note: she writes it was in Hamburg], Edith, who had been raised in a Jewish household, suddenly decided, as she herself put it, "not to pray anymore." Despite the fact that she was deeply impressed by the strict devotion of her mother, during her school and university years Edith slips into the intellectual world of atheism. She considers the existence of a personal God to be unworthy of belief.

In the years when she studied psychology, philosophy, history and German at the universities of Breslau, Göttingen and Freiburg, God didn't play an important role, at least initially. Her thinking was based on a demanding ethical idealism. In keeping with her intellectual abilities, she did not want to accept anything without careful examination, not even the faith of her fathers. She wanted to get to the bottom of things herself. As such, she was engaged in a constant search for the truth. Looking back on this period of intellectual unrest in her life she saw in it an important phase in a process of spiritual maturation. She said: "My search for the truth was a constant prayer." This is a comforting bit of testimony for those who have a hard time believing in God. The search for truth is itself in a very profound sense a search for God.

Under the influence of Edmund Husserl and his phenomenological school of thought the student Edith Stein became increasingly dedicated to the study of philosophy. She gradually learned to "view things free of prejudice and to throw off 'blinkers.'" She came into contact for the first time with Catholic ideas through a meeting with Max Scheler in Göttingen. She described her reaction to this meeting as follows: "The barriers of rationalistic prejudice, something I grew up with without being aware of it, fell and suddenly I was confronted with the world of faith. People I dealt with on a daily basis, people I looked up to in admiration, lived in that world."

Her long struggle for a personal decision to believe in Jesus Christ was not to come to an end until 1921 when she began to read the autobiographical Life of St. Teresa of Avila. She was immediately taken with the book and could not put it down until she had finished it. Edith Stein commented: "When I closed the book I said to myself: 'That is the truth!'" She had read through the night until sunrise. In that night she found truth–not the truth of philosophy, but rather the truth in person, the loving person of God. Edith Stein had sought the truth and found God. She was baptized soon after that and entered the Catholic Church.

### Continuing Heritage

7. For Edith Stein baptism as a Christian was by no means a break with her Jewish heritage. Quite the contrary, she said: "I had given up my practice of the Jewish religion as a girl of 14. My return to God made me feel Jewish again." She was always mindful of the

fact that she was related to Christ "not only in a spiritual sense, but also in blood terms." She suffered profoundly from the pain she caused her mother through her conversion to Catholicism. She continued to accompany her to services in the synagogue and to pray the psalms with her. In reaction to her mother's observation that it was possible for her to be pious in a Jewish sense as well, she answered: "Of course, seeing as it is something I grew up with."

Although becoming a member of the Carmelite order was Edith Stein's objective from the time of her encounter with the writings of St. Teresa of Avila, she had to wait more than a decade before Christ showed her the way. In her activity as a teacher and lecturer at schools and in adult education, mostly in Speyer, but also in Münster, she made a continuous effort to combine science and religion and to convey them together. In this she only wanted to be a "tool of the Lord." "Those who come to me I would like to lead to him," she said. During this period of her life she already lived like a nun. She took the vows privately and became a great and gifted woman of prayer. From her intensive study of the writings of St. Thomas Aquinas she learned that it is possible "to approach science from a religious standpoint." She said that it was only thus that she was able to decide to return seriously (after her conversion) to academic work. Despite her respect for scholarship, Edith Stein became increasingly aware that the essence of being a Christian is not scholarship, but rather love.

When Edith Stein finally entered the Carmelite order in Cologne in 1933, this step did not represent an escape from the world or from responsibility for her, but rather a resolved commitment to the heritage of Christ on the cross. She said in her first conversation with the prioress there: "It is not human activity that helps us—it is the suffering of Christ. To share in this is my desire." On being registered in the order she expressed the wish to be named "Blessed by the Cross." She had the words of St. John of the Cross printed on the devotional picture presented to her on taking her final vows: "My only vocation is that of loving more."

8. Dear brothers and sisters. We bow today with the entire church before this great woman whom we from now on may call upon as one of the blessed in God's glory, before this great daughter of Israel who found the fulfillment of her faith and her vocation for the

people of God in Christ the savior. In her conviction, those who enter the Carmelite order are not lost to their own—on the contrary they are won for them. It is our vocation to stand before God for everyone. After she began seeing the destiny of Israel from the standpoint of the cross, our newly beatified sister let Christ lead her more and more deeply into the mystery of his salvation to be able to bear the multiple pains of humankind in spiritual union with him and to help atone for the outrageous injustices in the world. As Benedicta a Cruce–blessed by the cross—she wanted to bear the cross with Christ for the salvation of her people, her church and the world as a whole. She offered herself to God as a "sacrifice for genuine peace" and above all for her threatened and humiliated Jewish people. After she recognized that God had once again laid a heavy hand on his people, she was convinced "that the destiny of this people was also my destiny."

### *His Suffering*

When Sister Teresa Benedicta of the Cross began her last theological work, *The Science of the Cross*, at the Carmelite convent in Echt (the work remained incomplete since it was interrupted by her own encounter with the cross) she noted: "When we speak of the science of the cross this is not. . .mere theory. . .but rather vibrant, genuine and effective truth." When the deadly threat to the Jewish people gathered like a dark cloud over her as well she was willing to realize with her own life what she had recognized earlier: "There is a vocation for suffering with Christ and by that means for involvement in his salvation. Christ continues to live and to suffer in his members. The suffering gone through in union with the Lord is his suffering, and is a fruitful part of the great plan of salvation."

With her people and "for" her people Sister Teresa Benedicta of the Cross traveled the road to death with her sister Rosa. She did not accept suffering and death passively, but instead combined these consciously with the atoning sacrifice of our savior Jesus Christ. A few years earlier she had written in her will: "I will gladly accept the death God chooses for me, in full submission to his holy will. I ask the Lord to accept my suffering and death for his honor and glory, and for all interests. . .of the holy church." The Lord heard her prayer.

### An Example

The church now presents Sister Teresa Benedicta a Cruce to us as a blessed martyr, as an example of a heroic follower of Christ, for us to honor and to emulate. Let us open ourselves up to her message to us as a woman of the spirit and of the mind, who saw in the science of the cross the acme of all wisdom, as a great daughter of the Jewish people and as a believing Christian in the midst of millions of innocent fellow men made martyrs. She saw the inexorable approach of the cross. She did not flee in fear. Instead, she embraced it in Christian hope with final love and sacrifice and in the mystery of Easter even welcomed it with the salutation *ave crux, spes unica.* As Cardinal Höffner said in his recent pastoral letter, "Edith Stein is a gift, an invocation and a promise for our time. May she be an intercessor with God for us and for our people and for all people."

9. Dear brothers and sisters, today the church of the 20th century is experiencing a great day. We bow in profound respect before the testimony of the life and death of Edith Stein, an outstanding daughter of Israel and, at the same time, a daughter of Carmel, Sister Teresa Benedicta of the Cross, a person who embodied a dramatic synthesis of our century in her rich life. Hers was a synthesis of a history full of deep wounds, wounds that still hurt, and for the healing of which responsible men and women have continued to work up to the present day. At the same time, it was a synthesis of the full truth on humankind, in a heart that remained restless and unsatisfied "until it finally found peace in God."

### Spirit and Truth

When we pay a spiritual visit to the place where this Jewish woman and Christian experienced martyrdom, the place of horrible events today referred to as *Shoah*, we hear the voice of Christ the Messiah and Son of Man, our Lord and Savior.

As the bearer of the message of God's unfathomable mystery of salvation he said to the woman from Samaria at Jacob's well:

"After all, salvation is from the Jews. Yet an hour is coming, and is already here, when authentic worshipers will worship the Father in spirit and truth. Indeed, it is just such worshipers the Father seeks. God is Spirit, and those who worship him must worship in spirit and truth" (Jn 4:22-24).

Blessed be Edith Stein, Sister Teresa Benedicta of the Cross, a true worshiper of God–in spirit and in truth. She is among the blessed. Amen.

Source: *L'Osservatore Romano,* Weekly Edition in English, no. 20, May 18, 1987, 19-20.

---

**STOP PRESS**

We note with great appreciation Pope John Paul II's declaration on October 1, 1999 of St. Teresa Benedicta of the Cross as co-patroness of Europe along with St. Bridget of Sweden and St. Catherine of Siena.

In his apostolic letter making the co-patronesses, the pope said the following, *inter alia,* about St. Teresa Benedicta: "With Edith Stein—St Teresa Benedicta of the Cross—we enter a very different historical and cultural context. For she brings us to the heart of this tormented century, pointing to the hopes which it has stirred, but also the contradictions and failures which have disfigured it. Unlike Bridget and Catherine, Edith was not from a Christian family. What we see in her is the anguish of the search and the struggle of an existential 'pilgrimage.' Even after she found the truth in the peace of the contemplative life, she was to live to the full the mystery of the Cross." [The Editor]

Source: *L'Osservatore Romano,* Weekly Edition in English, no. 40, October 6, 1999, 9.

# WASHINGTON
# COMMEMORATION

# Catholic University of America Welcome
## Ingrid Merkel

*In Gowan Hall Auditorium at 3:00pm Dr. Ingrid Merkel was introduced to the audience by the Commemoration coordinator, Fr. John Sullivan, OCD. Dr. Merkel offered the following words of welcome as Vice-Provost of the University.*

To you dear guests gathered here this afternoon to honor St. Teresa Benedicta of the Cross, Edith Stein, I bring greetings from President David O'Connell (currently in Rome) and from the entire community of The Catholic University of America. We are very grateful to be part of this celebration of the canonization of St. Teresa Benedicta of the Cross.

As a university community we have a special appreciation of the extraordinary example that Edith Stein holds up for us as a scholar who gave her life to the search for truth in no ordinary fashion. Her great intelligence, dedication, and persistence, let her shine as a *lumen universitatis* in the fulcrum of the movement of phenomenology, among great minds and mentors like Husserl and Max Scheler. In 1999, at the Catholic University of America and any other university, she would gain the recognition as a leading scholar that was denied her as a woman in the early decades of this century; she would receive promotion and tenure as a professor of philosophy.

But the constrictions imposed on her academic career never stopped Edith Stein from pursuing her goals. As a teacher of young women, as lecturer and writer she became a leader of the first rank in women's education. Stein's voice, trained in philosophical discourse, speaks lucidly and confidently of woman's natural gifts, professional competence and of woman's dignity.

But as a community of *faithful* scholars, what draws us most to this extraordinary thinker is her passage beyond the mere academic pursuit of truth to the realm where reason meets faith, in the words of our philosopher pope "Reason cannot eliminate the mystery of love which the cross represents, while the cross can give to reason the ultimate answer which it seeks" (*Fides et Ratio*, no. 23).

We are here assembled to commemorate the saint and martyr Teresa Benedicta of the Cross. It is in her martyrdom that Edith Stein's life became exemplary of the mystery of truth: "from the moment they speak to us of what we perceive deep down as the truth we have sought for so long, the martyrs provide evidence of a love that has no need of lengthy arguments in order to convince" (*Fides et Ratio*, no. 32).

On the fateful day August 2, 1942, upon their arrest by the S.S., Sr. Teresa Benedicta of the Cross comforted her sister Rosa: "Come Rosa, we go for our people." Her profound and unambiguous testimony to the universal message of the cross will be the crucible of this afternoon's dialogue.

If you would allow me a personal remark now: as a young child in the late 1940s I frequently attended Mass, vespers, or, in the month of May, the rosary in Sankt Maria vom Frieden, at the monastery of the community with which Sr. Teresa Benedicta lived from 1933 to 1938. I still remember the angelic voices of the sisters in the choir. Except for the Turn sister, we never saw them, we just heard their disembodied, heavenly voices. Edith Stein's memory as an outstanding member of the Carmelite community and as a saintly martyr had been kept very much alive in our community. I became familiar with the philosopher Edith Stein in the mid-fifties through my teacher, Sr. Agnes Bernharda, a Daughter of the Holy Cross and great admirer of Edith Stein who introduced us to her writings. It is with great joy and greater humility that I take part in the celebration today of this extraordinary woman.

# Saint Teresa Benedicta's Challenges for Our Times

**Eugene Fisher**

*Dr. Eugene Fisher has capably and sensitively represented the Catholic bishops of the United States to Jewish organizations for almost twenty years. He is a respected writer, speaker and thinker who oftentimes teams up with rabbis to produce significant catechetical tools to deepen understanding and mutual respect. He also assists the Vatican's council for Jewish religious matters as an international consultor.*

It is humbling to be honored by the invitation to participate in today's dialogue with Sue Batzdorff, niece of Edith Stein. Edith Stein represents so much about this century and her life coincided with so much of it. The topic at hand is not so much hagiographical as it represents the challenge that Edith Stein poses today to us Catholics. Susanne will undoubtedly delineate very clearly as she has done on several occasions, including articles in *America* magazine, ways to assist Catholics to understand the problematic that Edith Stein poses for the Jewish community. This has been very helpful for us in the church to begin to learn how to define what we really mean when we canonize a Jewish convert to Christianity. This raised, as anyone in the Jewish community could tell you, some very immediate questions. Two came to the fore, twelve years ago at the time of the beatification [in 1987], and they were addressed by the BCEIA rather amply. More recently, Cardinal Keeler, the episcopal moderator of the BCEIA of the National Conference of Catholic Bishops, has commented further about the canonization in the October 15, 1998 issue of *Origins*. It is very important to get this straight.

Canonizing a Jewish convert is not done very often. I am not aware of any direct precedents: of course St. Teresa of Avila was born into a Jewish *converso* family and became a doctor of the church, as should Edith Stein (in spite of the extra efforts the Discalced Carmelites will have to expend on that project), since she deserves to be a doctor of the church for her writings. Edith Stein's was a personal conversion and a personal journey which is the answer to one of the two major questions raised. The first of two questions that came immediately to Jewish persons was: Is this canonization of Edith Stein going to launch proselytizing activity? Is she going to become a model for what Catholics think Jews should do and what Jews should be, in line with the dictum "The only good Jew is a converted Jew"? Is that what this is all about? This question reveals the fact that the Jewish community does not have a whole lot of trust in the Catholic Church in terms of these matters of conversion, and for very good historical reasons. Anyone who reads the book of my [now deceased] predecessor, Father Edward Flannery, *The Anguish of the Jews*, will have ample testimony on why there is a certain thinness of trust in the Jewish community regarding Catholics. There have been many reasons for that over many centuries, for example, 1492's expulsion from Spain of the Jews who would not convert and then the subsequent Inquisition. In the latter case those Jews who submitted to forced conversion became subjects of the Inquisition because the Catholics (oftentimes led by political or economic considerations) felt these conversions might not be sincere. Aren't forced conversions seldom very sincere, anyway? Pope Gregory the Great, centuries before, realized that and forbade forced conversions under Canon Law that reigned for many centuries. Thus, the Spanish measures were in violation of Canon Law. The popes were much more successful in enforcing this in the Papal States than in Spain. Protests were tendered by Rome to Ferdinand and Isabella, but they did not listen at all to them. Had they listened to the pope subsequent Spanish history would have been quite different and much better. Those are the types of dynamics at work. Forced conversions continued into the 19th century. The last of the autos da fe, with burning Jews as heretics, took place in Mexico in the 1850s. This is not so long ago, historically: no wonder why the Catholic Church, immense as it is, lessens Jewish trust in it.

A friend of mine, Monsignor George Higgins, who taught here at Catholic University, says that to understand the Jewish-Catholic dialogue you have to imagine what happens if a mouse and an elephant were to sleep together in the same bed. The mouse might believe the elephant is his friend, but let the elephant turn to the wrong side in his sleep. . .that's it! We Catholics are, after a fashion, that elephant and gestures we think are small in themselves write large to those who historically have been so often on the wrong end of twitches, movements by the elephant.

Eleven years ago the bishops with their advisory statement urged Catholics to realize that in no way should the figure of Edith Stein ever be used as a tool for proselytizing Jews; nor should it be used as a model to promote among Catholics the idea that Jews *should* convert to Christianity as a matter of salvific necessity. That, actually, would be against church teaching. The Catholic Church fully respects the integrity of Judaism as a divinely revealed tradition. God's covenant with the Jewish people, we are told clearly by the Second Vatican Council, was never revoked by God. Jews should not even be disturbed at worship. Medieval Canon Law stated that anyone who disturbed Jews at worship would incur automatic excommunication because of that respect. Even with everything else going on, much of it very bad for the Jews during those centuries, this is a valid and true tradition.

Judaism is a response to a divine initiative and divine revelation. It is a religion we know for sure is based on direct, divine revelation. The record of that revelation is called the "Hebrew Scriptures." When in the 2nd century the church decided not to go along with Marcion's idea of getting rid of the Hebrew Scriptures, we decided that the basis of the Jewish faith is quite valid. So, there should be no question as to whether Jews who practice Judaism are going to heaven. Obviously, that is a divine promise and, if we believe in God's fidelity to God's promises, God will take care of the salvation of Jews. On the other hand, individuals—we Catholics would also affirm—have freedom of religion and God chooses people and gives them gifts of faith, sometimes in mysterious ways.

A little example I like to talk about is the parable of the two Pharisees who are presented in the Book of Acts [of the Apostles]. One Pharisee is totally closed to God, totally closed to the proclamation of Christ; so much so that he seeks ways to persecute Christians. He goes off on his horse along the road to Damascus: having cleaned out Jerusalem, he intends to "take care of" more of them. The other Pharisee stays in Jerusalem. Then, when the Apostles are arrested—all the Apostles, according to the Book of Acts—he rises and defends the right of these Christians to their religious freedom by the argument that, if this movement is not founded by God, it will fall apart under its own weight and, if it is, then God wants it to happen and one should let it go. So, the Apostles' lives were spared: the church's existence is owed to this person because the church could easily have been wiped out then, for our bishops are the successors of the Apostles, all of whom were under arrest. Who were the two Pharisees? While the persecutor closed to God was given the gift of faith, from a human point of view the other who seemed most open to the gift of faith remained faithfully Jewish. The latter was named Gamaliel, and he went on to be one of the rabbis who founded rabbinic Judaism. Go figure—this is God's will. And this is the relationship between us: Saul becomes St. Paul, and Gamaliel goes on to be one of the great rabbis of rabbinic tradition, one of the greatest teachers of Jewish history. Apparently this was God's will.

In our case we see the Jew Edith Stein responding, she believed and we Catholics agree with the honesty of her belief, responding to God's call to her. The implication of this, of course, as the bishops point out, is that Edith *is* a model *for Catholics*, she is *not* a model for Jews. The church presents her as a model for Catholics to emulate. This does not imply that other Jews need to follow her path, in terms of their own search for salvation. God's gift of faith is granted freely. In Edith Stein's case we believe her search for salvation had full integrity, and was one not influenced by any kind of force. In that particular university setting if she had wanted to impress her professors, she'd have wanted to become a Lutheran not a Catholic. Being the latter would not have given her an "in" in her university, nor did it enable her to overcome barriers against women, as pointed out by Dr. Ingrid Merkel. (Edith's image surely influences the question of feminism in the church.)

The second problem, forthrightly faced by the bishops, is the question as to what the church is actually doing in canonizing Edith Stein. All of a sudden it chooses one of six million Jews and declares her a martyr. Is she more a martyr than the rest of the others in the six million, the one million innocent Jewish children, because she happened to convert? What is the intention behind this? "Are you attempting," a Jew might ask, "to hint that the Holocaust was really a Catholic event, that they were primarily attacking Catholics and the primary victims were Catholics?" Everybody knows that the vast

majority of the murderer/executioners and the people who sup-
ported them were baptized Christians of various denominations:
that is, not all were Catholics, there were Lutherans and others in-
volved. So, what is the significance of that? The bishops were very
clear, along with the pope, to point out that what Catholics should
do when meditating on the significance of the life and death of
Edith Stein for the Catholic Church is learn to repent for what was
done to Jews by our fellow baptized Christians in Europe in the
dark days of the 1940s. Learn to repent. . .

Edith Stein's figure for us is a figure, not of triumphalism, not
of the church absorbing the Holocaust to make it our own, but a moment of repentance. This is how it should be celebrated liturgically,
how it should be understood. The pope said that every August 9
should be a day of repentance in the Catholic liturgical cycle. This
does not take away at all the importance of our remembering the
same theme, on the Sunday closest to Yom Hashoah [= Holocaust
Remembrance Day, April 13]. We can do this more than once a
year, for a theme as important as this, especially in the light of the
pope's call to repent at the turn of the millennium.

So Edith Stein is a reminder to us and will be a reminder to us,
and a constant goad to the Catholic Church. . .an annual goad and
wherever she is remembered more than once a year a constant goad
to our conscience: to remember what we did to her. "We" meaning
the Catholic Church, the community of the baptized which is beyond
the boundaries of the Catholic Church: the murderers were baptized.
They were not acting as Christians, but they were by and large baptized. They were framed in a European culture as the recent Vatican
document on the Holocaust puts it very strongly. They were framed
in a European culture that had been Christian for centuries and yet,
and yet, this Christian culture, this Christian people turned on its par-
ent tradition, its older brother or sister—however one defines the
sibling relationship that's there. And, of those who should have done
something, as the pope reminds us, very few did. Christians by and
large did not act, the pope said, during World War II toward their
Jewish brothers and sisters the way the world had every right to expect.
Among the reasons for that were the centuries of the "teaching of
contempt" against Jews and Judaism. The pope says that beginning
in the second century we Christians began to misinterpret and abuse

our own Bible, especially the New Testament, and turn it into a statement of collective guilt against Jews. Our God of Love, acting out of anger, we thought wanted to punish the Jews and destroy the Temple, as punishment for the alleged crime of deicide. Eventually this teaching turned the Jews into a protected but persecuted group within Christianity. That led to very negative attitudes toward Jews; negative attitudes compounded by scapegoated guilt. In 1096 the third wave of the First Crusade, the stragglers who did not make it along with their leaders to Jerusalem, slaughtered tens of thousands of Jews in what is today the Rhineland in Germany.

That was recorded with equal passion by both Catholic and Jewish chroniclers of the time. What didn't happen subsequent to 1096 was, however, communal self-reflection and repentance by Christians. What happened instead was a demonization of the Jews, as if to say "You were killed because you deserved it. It is your fault that we attacked you, not ours." That took us Christians off the hook. I tend to refer to "us Christians" so as to collectivize the matter; not to apply it to personal guilt but in terms of responsibility. We Christians, as the Vatican document on the Holocaust says, draw on, and not only take credit for, the merits of the saints (as parts of the body of the church)—and we underscore such merits by our commemoration today. But we also have to take responsibility for the sins of our fellow members: it's a package, we are one church in that sense. So we have to take responsibility: not as Americans, not as American Catholics because we both fled from Europe to America and our families sent relatives to fight Hitler. Still, we bear a sense of responsibility. That is why the pope and the Vatican document call upon us as a whole church to repent for what happened in the heart of Christendom in the 1940s. We are bound to our fellow baptized in this community, what Pius XII called the Mystical Body of Christ, the *communio*, the one community of faith.

These were the answers the bishops offered and that Cardinal Keeler reaffirmed very strongly, to two of the major questions. A third challenge for the church on how to understand Edith Stein is one not so susceptible to a clear answer. One can be very clear on the first two; the third presents greater difficulties because it is a little "fuzzy around the edges" in both communities. Let us put it this way: "Oh, you declare Edith Stein a martyr, but she was killed by the Nazis not because she was a Catholic but because she was a Jew." To that the pope agrees, but he adds she was also a Catholic martyr because what precipitated her being picked up was a very strong protest by the Dutch bishops in the face of warnings by the Nazis. The protest was against the deportation of Jews, and the response of the Nazis was to arrest all Jews, even those of just 1/8 Jewish origin. (Here in the U.S. we handle our race problem [poorly], not with Jews but with the one group of Americans who did not come here voluntarily, the African Americans. Something we haven't worked our way through, yet.) Catholics, then, of even 1/8 Jewish background were picked up and hauled away. Edith was one of them—a Jew to the Nazis, no more, no less. She was one of the six million, just another part of the "verminous" people that had to be cleansed out to have a pure Europe according to the sick Nazi ideology. That is true, and to the extent the beatification would lose sight of the Jewishness of Edith Stein, many Jewish people feared she would be declared solely a Catholic martyr and we would forget she was killed because she was a Jew in the eyes of the Nazis. So, the pope clearly declared she died "a daughter of Israel," she died as a Jew. On the other hand, there is another problematic issue challenging the Jewish community: this woman Catholics loved so much had left the way of the Jews and of their traditional religion, given them by God. What is Judaism? The word "Judaism" means the religion of the Jewish people. So, she left it and in so doing many in the Jewish community would argue, she could no longer claim the "law of return" in Israel or do other things consonant with membership in Judaism. This question "What is a Jew?" is very delicate. It is not something, however, the church can resolve: we can only accept at face value the integrity of Edith Stein's personal journey of faith and define the situation as best we can, rather than telling the Jewish community whether Edith Stein remained a Jew after her conversion. I think she felt she did; I think her family felt she did, some arguing one way, some another. From the point of view of the church that's enough; that is where we leave it. How the rabbinical groups and others in the Jewish community want to define what Judaism is and who is a Jew is really none of our business as Catholics. One must realize the delicacy of that situation. Rabbi Daniel Polish was very good, both in 1987 and more recently when he said the canonization

"serves to highlight one of the many areas of significant disagree-
ment between the Catholic Church and Jewish understanding. Thus,
while we cannot embrace the notion that Edith Stein will serve as a
bridge [which I have heard some Catholics contend because she
was a Jew and a Catholic], we can see the occasion of her canonization as opening a door to significant discourse. If this moment offers
us the opportunity to explore this area, it will have served a con-
structive purpose." This is a very significant insight.

I don't think we Catholics can single-handedly, from our side,
present Edith Stein to the Jewish community as a bridge of understanding, but she will always be an occasion for dialogue because
she is an occasion for self-reflection, for repentance by us and,
therefore, for reaching out to the Jewish community and to Judaism
as a living religion and tradition which we respect as divinely revealed, an occasion for dialogue and further understanding. With
that sort of careful, but necessary, framing Edith Stein becomes an
opportunity and will perpetually be an opportunity in the Catholic
liturgical calendar for outreach in dialogue to the Jewish community. A dialogue, furthermore, of mutual esteem and for recogniz-
ing fully the complete validity, on its own terms, of Judaism, the
faith of the Jewish people. This is, after all, the faith in which Jesus
Christ lived and died. . .there not being a Christianity to convert to
until the Resurrection. John the Baptist was not a Christian, nor were
the Maccabees, and yet we consider them to be saints. We need to
realize some very fundamental things about this. We have here a
very important ongoing challenge of the church. As a practitioner
of the dialogue I feel Edith Stein will be important in the long run
for Catholic-Jewish relations, even though it has caused some painful moments in the past year and some painful moments for both
Catholics and Jews back in 1987. I do not believe that the church will
move beyond the very strict understanding, one both the pope and
Cardinal Keeler following his lead have upheld, and abuse the figure of Edith Stein as a figure of conversionism or of triumphalism
about the Holocaust. Aware of literature issued by both the Edith Stein
Guild and religious education agencies in the church during the
last ten years I think she will serve to promote careful consideration
in a movement from Edith Stein to what killed Edith Stein, and who
killed Edith Stein and why she was killed. One reaches heightened

awareness, as a result, of a healthy Christian catechesis of the Holocaust, of the Shoah, of our need for repentance as a church.

My last point was to be the following: the significance of Edith Stein as a thinker and the ongoing significance, not simply of phenomenology (which may or may not survive the centuries) but of her feminism in her time. I mean by this not only her personal struggle but some of her writings and the way she framed issues: she was always part of an ongoing process, always at the cutting edge of the thinking of the time, so that the lesson we draw comes not just from what she said but from her role in the context of what she said ... like a constant goad. Dr. Merkel has already covered this ground admirably well.

To conclude: we need to think of Edith Stein's challenges in many ways; and I think we will meet them over the centuries as we move forward. We should realize she will probably be more significant in European and North American settings than in Asia or Africa. As for other places we await more efforts from the Carmelites to spread interest and consideration of these issues around the world where there is less attention paid to Catholic-Jewish relations than here in the United States. The figure of Edith Stein may help those countries recognize these issues. One final appeal: set about work to have Edith Stein declared a doctor of the church, because she really should be a doctor of the church as well as a martyr!

# Edith Stein's Challenges for Our Times
## Susanne Batzdorff

*Susanne Batzdorff identifies herself in the following text as the daughter of Erna, Edith Stein's closest and dearest sibling. Susanne receives clear and affectionately "honorable mention" in the autobiographical account of St. Teresa Benedicta titled "How I came to the Cologne Carmel." Perhaps no other family member has followed the steady growth in fame of Edith Stein with greater accuracy or keeness of intent. She is eminently qualified to reflect on this and related topics.*

Having listened attentively to Dr. Fisher's remarks, I am profoundly impressed with the fairness and balance of his presentation of a complex and controversial subject. To quote my great-aunt Emma, "With the best of intentions, I cannot say anything against him." Perhaps my role as a respondent can be understood as that of a member of a family from which Edith Stein is also descended. Edith Stein was the younger sister of my mother Erna, just one year and eight months younger than she. They were treated almost like twins, though they were very different. Erna, my mother, they said, was like clear water, while Edith was a book with seven seals. My mother lived to the age of almost 88 and thus was the last surviving sibling of seven. It was she who maintained contact with the various Carmelite communities and Catholic institutions who for a variety of reasons were interested in Edith Stein. My mother maintained a vast correspondence with persons all over the world who had questions about Edith or wanted some information. After my mother's death more than twenty years ago, these activities somehow fell into my lap. They have expanded and become an ongoing occupation. I have also translated and edited some of Edith Stein's writings and have spoken and written about her and about Catholic-Jewish dialogue.

I always preface my remarks with the caveat that, as a Jew and a close relative, my perspective is somewhat different from that of others to whom Edith Stein is a figure of admiration, veneration, even symbolism. To me, Aunt Edith is a very real person, someone whom I remember clearly and with great affection, who was loved, admired, and deeply mourned because of her untimely and cruel death. My mother was one of seven siblings, and only three were able to escape the Nazis. For our family Edith is not the symbol of the Holocaust. Her sister Rosa was murdered with her, on the same day and in the same bestial way. Her brother Paul and his wife were victims of the Nazis as was her sister Frieda and her niece Eva. We mourn them all and we cherish their memory. Word of the near certainty that Edith and Rosa Stein had perished reached my mother in a letter from Sr. Mechthildis of the Cologne Carmel dated April 14, 1947. It ends with the moving words, "Kind regards from the Cologne Carmel, which feels forever closely connected to you through your sister who was our sister, too."

When asked how she felt about Edith's impending canonization, Mother used to say: "I would a thousand times rather have a live sister than a dead saint." Just a few days ago, a cousin in Israel who read my book and who had never met Edith Stein reacted to her story with these words: "How I would have loved to know this interesting woman, and what a shame that the Nazis murdered her. . .It is so painful that this eminent and precious woman had to perish like that." So you see, ours is a somewhat different point of view.

I have never criticized the church for deciding to make my aunt a saint. The selection of candidates for sainthood is certainly the church's business. And yet it is a somewhat amazing notion to count a saint among one's relatives, particularly in a Jewish family. I do, however, have to come to terms with the question: Is she a bridge between Catholics and Jews or is she rather a hindrance in Jewish-Catholic dialogue? It seems that wherever we go, we encounter this question and find a whole range of responses. It is not surprising that Christians and Jews see things rather differently, but it is a challenge to us to engage in ongoing discussion to clarify our positions and to understand one another even if we cannot come to an agreement. The differences stem from the paradox of Edith Stein's life and death. After she became a Catholic, Edith Stein, in the words of Cardinal Keeler, "never for a moment felt that she had ceased to be a Jew." In the eyes of her Jewish family and the Jewish community from which she descended, with her conversion she ceased to be a Jew, though she always remained a beloved member of the family. That sounds harsh, but it is the way we see it.

I have described in various articles and books the reaction of our family at the time when my aunt entered the Carmelite order, the feeling of abandonment at a time of great distress. I have come to understand her spiritual journey after many years of pondering these matters, but this cannot change my conviction that someone who failed to find the answers to her spiritual quest in Judaism and embraces another faith can no longer claim to be a Jew. And thus I wince when the pope refers to my aunt as an eminent daughter of Israel. Such a daughter of our people can hardly be seen as a role model for Jews. I wonder whether someone born into the Catholic faith who decided to become a Jew or a Buddhist, would still be counted as a Catholic by the Catholic faith community. Or would Martin Luther still be regarded as a Catholic?

When we visited Wroclaw, the city of our birth and of Edith Stein's birth as well, we were invited to dinner at the home of Anita Stefanska, a member of the board of the Edith Stein Society of Wroclaw whose special portfolio is Catholic-Jewish relations. The president of the Society also attended and he sought our advice on how to approach the Jewish community there to establish friendly relations with them. "We invite them to our meetings and celebrations, but we always meet with a rebuff. They don't want to have anything to do with us. They seem to be suspicious of us."

Harsh though it may have sounded, we had to tell them: "You may be proud of Edith Stein, but Jews see her primarily as someone who left Judaism and became a Christian." We suggested to these good and very sincere people that it might work better if they found common projects to work on together with the Jewish group, projects that had nothing to do with the saint after whom the society is named and that could bring the two groups together for positive cooperation and mutual benefit. I wish them success. Edith Stein may not serve as a bridge; she may rather open a door to allow Christians and Jews to see each other, to learn about each other, to become familiar without having to merge and to lose our identity in the process.

Ironically Edith Stein, who became a Christian, was defined by the Nazis as a Jew, for she came from Jewish parents. The fact of her baptism made no difference to her persecutors, and they killed her along with the millions of others, regardless of whether they were devout Jews or marginal Jews or had become Christians, devout or otherwise.

So why did I choose to attend this event, and why did so many relatives go to Rome? Actually, for me this was not such a difficult decision as it had been eleven years earlier. Then, one could not escape the impression that this act was an attempt to make up for the failings of the church during the Holocaust. A Jewish martyr of the Holocaust who is at the same time a martyr for the church was a confusing and disturbing image. And the sad failure of the church leadership during the Holocaust could not be compensated by picking a Jewish-born Catholic for beatification. Nevertheless I went, for the love of my aunt, who was a great human being, who never forgot her Jewish connections and roots and always remained in solidarity with the Jewish people. She never attempted to proselytize among members of her family or friends.

In spring 1933, when few people took Hitler's rantings seriously and many dismissed him as a "clown," my aunt Edith wrote to the reigning pope, Pius XI, to urge him to issue an encyclical against the evil of anti-Semitism. It was a courageous attempt to use her position as a Jewish-born Catholic, a prominent lecturer and scholar to admonish the church hierarchy to take its moral leadership position seriously. Sadly her voice was not heard; there was no response. We have often speculated on how history might have been affected, had the two Piuses taken a different stand in those early months of National Socialism. When the pope concluded an agreement, the ominous Concordat, with the National Socialist government, antifascists and Jews in Germany were shocked and bitterly disappointed. While, as I said before, I believe that it is the church's exclusive domain whom to select for beatification or canonization, I feel certain that, if such honors were bestowed on Pius XII, who, after all, implemented that treaty, it would seriously set back Catholic-Jewish rapprochement, which we are so earnestly pursuing.

Edith Stein's beatification was for me also a memorial for Edith and her sister Rosa, who had no burial, no grave, no period of mourning. I went for the love of my mother, who, I was sure, would have attended, had she lived. And I went for my Jewish people, to bear witness that there are devout Jews in Edith Stein's family, that Hitler could not destroy us all and that he could not do away with Jewish life. Those reasons, for me, were good and sufficient.

When it came time to make those same decisions for the canonization, I had an additional reason: The present pope's actions over the past years have demonstrated his sincere desire to improve relations with the Jews and with Israel. Though an outright apology for the silence of the Vatican during the Holocaust has not occurred, many steps have been taken to insure that such attitudes will never prevail in the future.

With his facility in many languages and his willingness to travel the globe, even now, at the age of 78 and in ill health, Pope John Paul II has managed to build bridges where hitherto seemingly unbridgeable gulfs existed. When controversy arose concerning the establishment of a Carmelite monastery adjacent to the death camp of Auschwitz, the pope saw to it that this monastery was moved.

In 1986, Pope John Paul II paid a visit to the great synagogue of Rome, the first pope ever to go there. In 1993, he established diplomatic relations between the Vatican and Israel. And in 1994, he sponsored a concert at the Vatican, commemorating the Shoah.

In addition, there was another powerful incentive for going to Rome: While in 1987 our family delegation had numbered less than 25, it developed that almost 100 family members would gather in Rome for this event. It was an awesome prospect not to be missed. We found on this occasion relatives from four continents, representing four generations. They represented a veritable United Nations and, though most were probably Jewish, some were Catholics and others Protestants. We took no census, delighting merely in the fact that we had this grand opportunity to connect with such a large representation of family members. Hitler had vowed to destroy us, and the Nazi persecution had scattered us in all directions. Yet here we were, uniting to honor a member of our family whom few of those present had known personally, and discovering our common roots and bonds. To me this extended family of Edith Stein is a microcosm of the world. Like this family, we human beings must bridge our differences and find the common ground that will enable us to work together for the good of our world. And I can't help thinking that such a gathering in her honor would please my aunt, who cherished her family.

Edith Stein challenges our times in many ways, just as she challenged her own time. She relentlessly pursued the truth as she saw it. In her search she did not hesitate to deviate from the path of her family, which a more conventional, less determined seeker might have followed. She left the faith of her ancestors, even though it meant a very painful rupture in family harmony. Even though she was a newcomer to the Catholic faith, she investigated the role of women in religious as well as secular society and was not afraid to reveal the conclusions she arrived at. Long before she found her path of faith, she joined the struggle for women's political and civic emancipation. She recognized that women are not defined solely by their gender, but have individual gifts and talents just as men do. They should not be regarded as merely wives and mothers. Her lectures made a profound impression on European audiences between the two world wars, but even today, much of what she taught is timely and valid. She was never shrill or confrontational. A school teacher listening to her describes her demeanor thus:

> She spoke unrhetorically, with quiet charm, using clear, attractive, unpretentious words. Despite this you immediately sensed a tremendous strength of intellect and an extremely rich, intensely disciplined interior life springing from absolute conviction. She neither accused, disputed, nor threatened. She simply stated the facts, and, in the course of her presentation, the dangers facing our nation became startlingly clear.

Some of her teachings have yet to be considered or seriously investigated by the secular society and by the church. Far be it from me to set myself up as an expert on what the role of women in the Catholic Church should be, but I think I have already noticed that the role of the nun has expanded since the days when my aunt Edith entered Carmel. While her activities were a rare exception, today it is quite acceptable for a Carmelite nun to take up literary or scholarly work. Many Carmelite sisters I have met demonstrate by the lives they lead that creative activities are entirely compatible with their religious vocation.

Whether future developments within the church may open up the possibility of women as priests remains an open question. In her essay "The Separate Vocations of Man and Woman according to Nature and Grace" she states:

> . . .feminine energies are now strongly demanded as help in church charities and pastoral work. In recent militant movements, the women are demanding that their activities be recognized once

more as an ordained church ministry, and it may well be that one day attention will be given to their demands. Whether this will be the first step then, finally, on the path leading to women in the priesthood is the question. It seems to me that such an implementation by the church, until now unheard of, cannot be forbidden by dogma.

The present pope has certainly not embraced such a development, but the issue has not gone away.

In 1933, in a time of danger she was not content to sit on the sidelines, but attempted to take action. What a bold idea it was to try to gain a private audience with the pope in order to urge him to take a lead which might have been of profound significance. In this, too, I see a challenge for our own times. Do not refrain from acting in a righteous cause just because your one voice may not be powerful enough. Speak out when a wrong is being committed. One voice can be more powerful than we think.

For me the path of my aunt Edith has actually provided a push toward more intensive involvement with Judaism. What she rejected, I felt impelled to learn more about, to delve into my Jewish heritage, to make it truly my own, so that I might say, with equal conviction, "This is the truth." I am not sure whether I shall ever get there. At this point I am prepared to admit that there are many truths. I am willing to grant that Edith Stein found hers elsewhere. But I am confident that my truth will remain in Judaism.

Father Victor Donovan, my ninety-year-old ecumenical pen-pal has said that if Edith Stein can be the means for promoting fruitful dialogue between our two religions and if we can thereby arrive at a more harmonious relationship, she will have achieved a greater miracle than that for which she was canonized. I feel that the miracle can only be achieved by us, Christians and Jews, talking to each other, working together and thus bringing about the progress we all say we desire. Edith Stein may be a catalyst, but it is to ourselves that we must look to work the miracle.

If we examine our past and admit our mistakes honestly, we can go forward confidently and work together for common goals. And with God's blessing we can go about the task of *tikkun olam*, repairing the world.

# Homily at Evening Prayer
## John Sullivan

*His Eminence William Cardinal Keeler had accepted the Carmelites'
invitation to preside and preach the homily at Evening Prayer but he was
impeded from attending by a storm that brought five inches of snow to
Mount Saint Mary s Seminary where he was staying. Very Rev. Fr. Phillip
Thomas, OCD, ultimate sponsor of the afternoon's activities as Provincial
of the Discalced Carmelites, took the cardinal's place presiding at the ceremonies and Fr. John Sullivan, OCD gave the following reflection:*

Allow me one remark to frame my presence before you instead
of Cardinal Keeler here in the crypt church of the Basilica of the National Shrine of the Immaculate Conception. We included a poem
of St. Teresa Benedicta in this evening's prayer service that is a translation by Sue Batzdorff, present here among us along with her husband Al and their cousins Howard and Holly Stein. This choice was
really not made to provide an extra "bouquet" to Sue for her partici-
pation in today's activities honoring her aunt, but at this moment its
choice seems more and more appropriate and prophetic, since in
stanza three of that poem "At the Helm" the new saint says: "Through
stormy night you'll cross the deep / 'twill help you to steer true."
Looking forward to today no one thought that in mid-March in Washington we would have a truly "stormy night," but all the snow and
sleet outside has indeed changed the "line-up" in this prayer service
designed to commemorate Edith Stein and all victims of the unjust
persecution they suffered at the hands of the Nazis.

The text of Holy Scripture just proclaimed was taken from
Evening Prayer II for *Laetare* Sunday and read as follows:

> "While all the runners in the stadium take part in the race, the award
> goes to only one. In that case, run so as to win! Athletes deny them-
> selves all sorts of things. They do this to win a crown of leaves that
> withers, but we a crown that is imperishable." (1Co 9:24-25)

This celebration in thanksgiving links us to a significant, portentous event in St. Edith Stein's life.

In a multi-faceted commemoration like this my Order, the Discalced Carmelites, wishes to show gratitude to the hierarchy of our church for the church-wide declaration that Edith Stein is a saint, worthy of imitation. That is why we had invited Cardinal Keeler to join us in prayer; and why Bishop William Lori, representing Cardinal Hickey, was with us earlier to give the invocation at the dialogue held at the pontifical Catholic University of America. They reflect, after a fashion, the significant gesture of other bishops made near the end of her life.

Back in 1942 the Bishops of Holland, where she was staying, not so far from her home monastery in Cologne, rose up in indignation against the anti-Semitic policies of the Nazi occupiers of that country. In all the Catholic churches, on a Sunday like today, they ordered the reading of a pastoral letter telling everyone how unjust the treatment of all the Jews in Holland was, as the Nazis were intensifying their demonic efforts to apply the infamous "final solution" that brought millions of innocent Jews to their unmerited deaths.

Sr. Teresa Benedicta or Edith Stein's own death was precipitated by a round-up that was decreed as a reprisal against those courageous bishops as they tried desperately to bring the German armed forces in Holland to their senses.

Of course, had she not been arrested that way, we are told by the experts in the Vatican, Edith Stein would not have been beatified or canonized as a Catholic martyr, and perhaps we would all be awaiting further progress still on her cause for beatification. As it is, she was beatified a martyr in 1987; and a miracle certified, with the technical assent of the Jewish doctor who took care of the sick little girl cured through the intercession of Edith Stein, brought her to last October's canonization ceremony that we are commemorating this afternoon. All this because a group of bishops more than a half-century ago stood up to injustice.

Is this not an important lesson to be gained from the reading we have just heard? The Apostle Paul talks of competition. Very interestingly, the word for competition he used in his native Greek was *agonia*. That word has become agony, and means struggle too. To assure justice so often it takes a struggle, so that those who agonize as victims of injustice may be freed from their unwarranted situation.

I say this so we commemorate, yes, but not just comfortably and surely *not* triumphalistically.

We commemorate Edith Stein, Sr. Teresa Benedicta of the Cross, for her "contributions," the word chosen by Doctor Ronald Kleinman when, appearing on the ABC television network, he described her significant life. These were her philosophy studies; her service in World War I as a Red Cross volunteer; her many years of teaching; her life in community aimed always at breaking down barriers, promoting harmony, fostering tolerance. She contributed them as she offered herself to others.

May we take inspiration from her and do our utmost to provide a future full of contributions designed to help others, and one free from the *agonia* she suffered.

# Edith Stein: A Fragmented Life

## Steven Payne

*Fr. Steven Payne is current editor of the Collected Works of Edith Stein for ICS Publications. The following article he contributed to the news weekly* America *received a first-place award from the Catholic Press Association of North America as "Best Personality Profile" of 1998.*

[magazine introduction]

*At an open-air ceremony in the Cologne soccer stadium on May 1, 1987, Pope JohnPaul II beatified Edith Stein, that is, he declared her worthy of public veneration as a genuinely holy, or blessed, person.*

*In Rome on Oct. 11, the Pope will canonize Edith Stein, who was known in the Carmelite order as Sister Teresa Benedicta of the Cross, proclaiming her a saint.*

*In the following essay, Steven Payne, O.C.D., provides an overview of the new saint's life and reflections upon certain aspects of its significance. Father Payne is the prior of the Discalced Carmelite monastery in Washington, D.C., and an instructor at the Washington Theological Union. He is also editor-in-chief of the Institute of Carmelite Studies Publications, which includes among its current projects the publication of English translations of the collected works of Edith Stein. This article is based on a homily the author gave at the Baltimore Carmel on Aug. 9.*

The canonization of Edith Stein will no doubt bring, along with further arguments over her status as a martyr, a growing chorus of praise for her remarkable achievements. Yet despite the accolades, we know that her life could hardly be considered a success story by any ordinary standards. Perhaps it is her very failures that bring her closer to us. Certainly there is no denying Edith Stein's gifts and accomplishments, for they were many. Still more striking are the innumerable separations, setbacks and disappointments she endured and the countless unexpected turns her journey took.

These speak eloquently of the struggle to find meaning in the loose ends that compose our lives. Scarcely anything turned out exactly as she anticipated except, ironically, her death at the hands of the Nazi regime. We have the advantage of hindsight and can glimpse, through the seeming chaos of her life, the hand of God guiding her to a great destiny. But surely the way must have been very dark for her as she was traversing it.

The disappointments began even in childhood. Only two years after her birth in Breslau in 1891 as the youngest child in a large Jewish family, Edith's father died suddenly at the age of 48, leaving behind her mother, Auguste Stein, to manage a failing lumberyard and raise seven children on her own. Though Auguste soon made the family business prosper—some called her the best businessman in Breslau—this surely limited the time she could spend with her own children. Yet Edith's relationship with her mother became the strongest emotional bond in her life, which made it all the more painful later when Auguste could not accept Edith's conversion to Christianity.

Edith was a bright, precocious and sometimes headstrong child. "In my dreams," she wrote in her autobiography with more than a hint of self-mockery, "I always foresaw a brilliant future for myself. I dreamed about happiness and fame for I was convinced that I was destined for something great and that I did not belong at all in the narrow, bourgeois circumstances into which I had been born." [Edith Stein wrote this autobiography, an unfinished memoir of her life up to 1916, between 1933 and 1935 after she had entered the Carmelite order. The German original was published posthumously in 1985. An English translation appeared the following year under the title *Life in a Jewish Family* (I.C.S. Publications: Washington, D.C.).]

## School Years

At the age of six she insisted on being admitted early to the Victoria School in Breslau and was indignant at being sent to kindergarten first. By 13 she thought she had enough of academics and dropped out of school. She returned to studies after only a few months' absence, but already we can see the intellectual restlessness that would mark her whole life. It was at this time also, she admits, that she made a conscious decisionto give up praying and walked away from the devout Jewish faith of her beloved mother.

She entered the University of Breslau in 1911 to study psychology, but was disappointed with the approach of her professors who were part of a movement at that time trying to reduce psychology to an exact empirical science, like physics and chemistry. "I came to feel that Breslau had nothing more to offer me," she writes. "Something was pushing me to move on." She had heard of the growing reputation of a philosophy professor in Göttingen, Edmund Husserl (1859–1938), who was developing a new phenomenological method that promised to clarify the foundations of all thought and experience. With a sense of intense intellectual excitement, coupled with the great pain of leaving her mother behind in Breslau, she transferred schools and became a vital part of the so-called Göttingen Circle, a group of Husserl's students who would go on to become famous philosophers in their own right.

Yet here again things did not turn out as she had hoped. A warm friendship with a handsome young philosopher named Hans Lipps never developed into the romance that some expected. When writing her dissertation, at times she became so frustrated and depressed that, as she wrote, "I could no longer cross the street without wishing I would be run over by some vehicle. And when we went on an excursion, I hoped I would fall off a cliff and not return alive."

World War I interrupted university life, and while she bravely volunteered for nursing duty, some of her closest philosophical associates were dying at the front. She tells us how, at one point, she went to console the widow of one of her favorite professors, Adolf Reinach, who had been killed in battle on Nov. 16, 1917. She was surprised to find herself consoled instead by Anna Reinach's great faith. Experiences like this began to make her rethink her casual dismissal of religion. Yet her struggles continued.

Following Husserl to Freiburg, she finally completed her doctorate in 1916, summa cum laude, with a dissertation "on the problem of empathy." This was a critical issue in phenomenology, since it has to do with how we are able to know anything at all about the inner life of other persons. After this promising start, she offered to become Husserl's assistant, and he happily agreed. This required her to take the revered master's loose papers and manuscripts, written in shorthand, and try to decipher and organize them into some kind of coherent whole. Yet once again she met only with frustration, because she could seldom get Husserl to review the edited texts she had so painstakingly stitched together. A brilliant academic future might have seemed assured. But things turned out otherwise. No German university was yet ready to have a female philosophy professor on its full-time faculty, and in fact Husserl's letter of recommendation was less enthusiastic than it should have been. Later on, as Marianne Sawicki has recently noted, Martin Heidegger would publish some of the same Husserl manuscripts Edith Stein had worked on as if he himself had been their editor (Sawicki, *Body, Text and Science: The Literacy of Investigative Practices and the Phenomenology of Edith Stein* [Dordrecht: Kluwer, 1997]). Yet nowhere do we find Edith complaining that others are taking credit for her work.

*Conversion and Entry Into Carmel*

It was at about this time that she had her famous conversion experience after reading the autobiography of St. Teresa of Avila. She is supposed to have read the book during the course of a single night in 1921. When she closed it she declared, "This is truth!" She had finally discovered the truth she had been seeking, not in the works of famous philosophers or theologians, but in the autobiography of another woman of Jewish ancestry who, in the face of great adversity, had found both herself and her God. Stein would later say that her search for truth was itself a kind of prayer, and that "those who seek the truth seek God, whether they realize it or not."

Edith's baptism on Jan. 1, 1922, provoked new conflicts and misunderstandings with her friends and family. Her mother was heartbroken. Fritz Kaufmann (1891–1958), himself a Jew and one of Edith's closest friends from the Göttingen circle, cut off communication with her for some years, and was only won back by Edith's persistence. As she explained, once she admitted people into her friendship, she never let them go.

From 1923 to 1931 she taught in a Dominican teachers' college in Speyer, and from 1932 to 1933 at the German Institute for Scientific Pedagogy in Münster. She excelled, but these jobs were far below what her talents and training would have warranted. With the rise of National Socialism, more and more doors were closed to her and other Jews. For a time, she was still able to serve as a leader in the Catholic Women's Movement. She translated Thomas Aquinas's *Disputed Questions on Truth* and tried to reconcile phenomenology with Catholic thought, although many of the scholastic philosophers and theologians of her time were critical of her efforts. In 1933 she had planned to travel to Rome, as she tells us, "to ask the Holy Father in a private audience for an encyclical" against Nazi anti-Semitism. Instead, she was only able to send Pius XI a letter that was delivered but never answered. We can only imagine the impact if the Pope had heeded her advice. But once again her courageous and far-sighted efforts seemed to come to nothing.

In October of that same year, she entered the Carmel of Cologne. She requested and received a religious name that reflected not only her love for the great founding figures of the Discalced Carmelites, Teresa of Avila and John of the Cross, but her growing understanding, in faith, of her own dark and peculiar path. She became Teresia Benedicta a Cruce (Teresa Blessed by the Cross). More and more she would be drawn into what she would later call *Kreuzeswissenschaft*, the "science of the cross," the mystery of joy in suffering, of victory in failure, of dying and rising with Christ.

In an essay on "Love of the Cross" she wrote: "To suffer and to be happy although suffering, to have one's feet on the earth, to walk on the dirty and rough paths of this earth and yet to be enthroned with Christ at the Father's right hand, to laugh and cry with the children of this world and ceaselessly sing the praises of God with the choirs of angels—this is the life of the Christian until the morning of eternity breaks forth."

Her family, especially her mother, was deeply wounded when she became a nun and viewed her decision as a kind of betrayal of her own people in their deepest hour of need. Yet Edith had discovered a precedent in the Hebrew Scriptures for her mysterious calling. She wrote from Cologne on Oct. 31, 1938, after the death of her mother, about the sufferings of her family as they tried to emigrate: "If only [my family] knew where to go! But I trust that, from eternity, Mother will take care of them. And [I also trust] in the Lord's having accepted my life for all of them. I keep having to think of Queen Esther who was taken from among her people precisely so that she might represent them before the king. I am a very poor and powerless little Esther, but the King who chose me is infinitely great and merciful. That is such a great comfort."

Edith felt in her heart, in a way she could never adequately explain, that she was giving her life for others. That is, in fact, how she tried to articulate her vocation to an uncomprehending Fritz Kaufmann in a letter of May 14, 1934: "Whoever enters Carmel is not lost to her own, but is theirs fully for the first time; it is our vocation to stand before God for all."

### Writing and Auschwitz

While she continued writing within the walls of Carmel, she keenly felt the lack of time and scholarly resources in her new environment, as well as the gaps in her intellectual formation. Nazi policies prevented many of her works from this period, including her masterpiece, *Finite and Eternal Being,* from appearing in print. Some of her letters now preserved in the archives of the State University of New York at Buffalo are poignant pleas for help in getting that book published in the United States. More than 50 years after her death this has yet to be done, partly because of posthumous fights over her literary remains.

It is a striking fact that Edith's most important works, like all the great Carmelite classics, were written not within the protective environment of a university campus but in the midst of a religious community, with its constant demands and interruptions. In a sense, we can see her as a model for the many women and men who have to pursue scholarship and find their voice outside the customary academic channels.

Given these circumstances, one can well understand why she wrote so often and with so much feeling about the struggle of coping with a fragmented life. "What did not lie in my plans," she said in words often quoted, "lay in God's plans." And elsewhere she wrote: "When night comes, and retrospect shows that everything was patchwork and much which one had planned [is] left undone, when so many things rouse shame and regret, then take all as it is, lay it in God's hands, and offer it up to him. In this way we will be able to rest in him, actually to rest, and to begin the new day like a new life."

As the Nazi threat increased, she was finally forced to flee to the Carmel in Echt,Holland, on New Year's Eve in 1938. This move was largely to spare the nuns in Cologne from any reprisals they might have suffered for harboring a Jewish nun. But the safe haven was only temporary. After Germany invaded Holland, and in retaliation for a July 1942 letter by the Dutch bishops criticizing Nazi policies, Edith Stein was arrested along with her sister Rosa, who lived in the Echt Carmel, and other Catholics of Jewish descent. They were deported to Auschwitz, where Edith Stein died in the gas chambers on Aug. 9, 1942. Almost the last words heard from her as she was being led away from the Echt Carmel were addressed to her distraught sister: "Come, Rosa, we are going for our people!"

Even in death, her troubles were not over. The church's decision to honor Edith Stein as a martyr has made her a "sign of contradiction" for many Jews today, who fear that Catholics are thereby attempting to co-opt the Holocaust. Surely a woman whose Christian faith only increased her appreciation of her Jewish roots, and who worked tirelessly to improve mutual understanding between Christians and Jews, could only be pained by such disputes. Surely she wanted to be a bridge rather than a stumbling block. We must hope, with her, that these current controversies will be the prelude to a deeper dialogue.

By worldly standards, then, hers was not a triumphant life or death. None of the glorious dreams of her childhood had been fulfilled. To those without faith, Edith Stein's story surely looks like a series of false starts and frustrated hopes. Even today she has not yet received the recognition she deserves for her contributions to feminism, phenomenology, educational theory, Catholic thought and inter-religious dialogue. She did not live to see the fruits of her self-sacrifice. But out of all the apparent failures and disappointments, out of all the disjointed fragments of her life, God wove a great tapestry and accomplished a great work.

For those who might consider such a life a failure, let the final word be that of Fritz Kaufmann, one of her friends from student days in Göttingen. After Hitler came to power, Kaufmann emigrated to the United States, where he taught philosophy at what is now the

State University of New York at Buffalo. On Sept. 9, 1945, after receiving word of Edith Stein's fate, he wrote a letter that is preserved in the SUNY Buffalo archives. In it he said:

> I am disconsolate at Edith Stein's death though I am still hoping—perhaps, against hope—that the news will not prove true. With Hans Lipps and her my best Göttingen friends are gone, and life seems so much poorer. It is as if a door to a beloved room of the past had been definitely locked. You can hardly imagine what [Edith Stein] meant to me during the first World War when she did everything to keep me spiritually alive and abreast with the intellectual events within our movement and outside. She was the kind genius of our whole circle, taking care of everything and everybody with truly sisterly love (also of Husserl who was seriously ill in 1918). She was like a guardian angel to Lipps in the years of his distress. When I spoke to her last time in the Cologne monastery—a lattice between her room and mine—the evening twilight made her fade to my eyes: I felt I was not to see her again. But who could have thought that these beasts would not stop in their cruelty even before a nunnery, and that she would have to die as she may have done? She had joined the Carmelites' order on account of her special veneration for Santa Theresa, but also because she wanted to offer her life and her prayers, in this ascetic community, to save mankind. Did she succeed, after all, in this highest task?

Source: *America*, October 10, 1998, 11–14.

# FOR FURTHER READING

## ENGLISH TRANSLATIONS OF EDITH STEIN'S WORKS

*Essays on Woman,* tr. of *Die Frau* by Freda Mary Oben. Collected Works of Edith Stein, 2. Washington, DC: ICS Publications, 1987; revised edition 1997.

*The Hidden Life, Essays, Meditations, Spiritual Texts,* tr. of *Verborgenes Leben* by Waltraut Stein. Collected Works of Edith Stein, 4. Washington, DC: ICS Publications, 1992.

*Life in a Jewish Family,* tr. of *Aus dem Leben einer jüdischen Familie* by Josephine Koeppel. Collected Works of Edith Stein, 1. Washington, DC: ICS Publications, 1986.

*The Mystery of Christmas,* tr. of *Das Weihnachtsmysterium* by Josephine Rucker. Darlington, England: Carmelite Press, 1985.

*On the Problem of Empathy,* tr. of *Zum Problem der Einfühlung* by Waltraut Stein. The Hague Martinus Nijhoff, 2nd ed., 1970. Revised ed.: Collected Works of Edith Stein, 3. Washington, DC: ICS Publications, 1989.

*The Science of the Cross,* tr. of *Kreuzeswissenschaft* by Hilda C. Graef. Chicago: Regnery, 1960. [out of print; new trans. from ICS Publications near completion in 1999]

*Self-Portrait in Letters,* tr. of *Selbstbildnis in Briefen* by Josephine Koeppel. Collected Works of Edith Stein, 5. Washington, DC: ICS Publications, 1993.

"Ways to Know God," tr. of *Wege der Gotteserkenntnis* by Rudolf Allers, *The Thomist* 9 (1946), 379-420. Reprinted as an Edith Stein Guild Publication, New York, 1981.

*Writings of Edith Stein,* selected, translated, and introduced by Hilda C. Graef. Westminster, MD: The Newman Press, 1956. [out of print]

"How I came to the Cologne Carmel" etc. in *Edith Stein: Selected Writings: with Comments, Reminiscences and Translations of her Prayers and Poems by her Niece,* tr. by Susanne M. Batzdorff. Springfield, IL: Templegate Publishers, 1990.

## STEIN WORKS FORTHCOMING FROM ICS PUBLICATIONS

*Contributions to Philosophical Foundation of Natural and Human Sciences,* tr. Mary Catherine Baseheart & Marianne Sawicki

*Finite and Eternal Being,* tr. Kurt Reinhardt

*Knowledge and Faith,* tr. Walter Redmond

*Science of the Cross,* tr. Josephine Koeppel

## SELECTED BOOKS AND ARTICLES

"Advisory on the Implications for Catholic-Jewish Relations of the Beatification of Edith Stein," April 24, 1987. Washington: Secretariat for Catholic-Jewish Relations, Bishops' Committee for Ecumenical and Interreligious Affairs, NCCB, 1987. 1 p.

Baseheart, Mary Catherine. *Person in the World: Introduction to the Philosophy of Edith Stein.* Dordrecht, Boston, London: Kluwer Academ. Publishers, 1997. "Contributions to Phenomenology," 27.

Batzdorff. Susanne. *Aunt Edith: The Jewish Heritage of a Catholic Saint.* Springfield, IL: Templegate Publishers, 1998.

____. "Aunt Edith: Jewish Heritage, Catholic Saint," *America* 180 (February 13, 1999), 15–16, 18–20, 22–23.

____. "Remembering Edith: A Conversation with Susanne M. Batzdorff," *Reform Judaism* 27 (1999), 33-36.

Biberstein, Ernest with Michael Biberstein. "A Protest Unacknowledged," *Reform Judaism* 27 (1999), 30–32.

____. "Open Letter to John Paul: Speak the Whole Truth about Christians and the Holocaust," *National Catholic Reporter* 35 (October 23, 1998), 22.

Carroll, James. "The Saint and the Holocaust: Has the Vatican rewritten the Life of Edith Stein?", *The New Yorker* 75 (June 7, 1999), 52–57.

Gordon, Mary, "Saint Edith?", *Tikkun* 14 (1998), 17–20.

Kavanaugh, Kieran. "The Canonization Miracle and Its Investigation," in *Never Forget: Catholic and Jewish Perspectives on Edith Stein,* Carmelite Studies 7, pp. 185-96. [see S. Payne below]

Keeler, James (Cardinal). "Advisory addresses Jewish Concerns about the Canonization of Edith Stein, *Origins* 28 (October 15, 1998), 301, 303–05.

Meier, Lynn. "Empathy as Means," *Spiritual Life* 44 (1998), 131–36.

Neyer, Sr. Maria Amata. *Edith Stein: Her Life in Photos and Documents,* tr. Waltraut Stein. Washington, DC: ICS Publications, 1999.

Oben, Freda Mary. "A Witness for Christians and Jews," *Inside the Vatican* 6 (October 1998), XII–XV.

Payne, Steven. "Edith Stein and John of the Cross," *Teresianum* 50 (1999, 1–2), 239–56.

____. US ed. *Never Forget: Christian and Jewish Perspectives on Edith Stein,* tr. Susanne Batzdorff. Washington, DC: ICS Publications, 1998. "Carmelite Studies," 7.

Sawicki, Marianne. *Body, Heart, and Science: The Literacy of Investigative Practices and the Phenomenology of Edith Stein.* Dordrecht, Boston, London: Kluwer Academ. Publishers, 1997. "Phaenomenologica," 144.

Schlafke, Jakob. *Edith Stein, Documents concerning her Life and Death,* tr. Susanne M. Batzdorff. New York: Edith Stein Guild, 1984.

Signer, Michael. "An Irresistible Choice," *Reform Judaism* 27 (1999), 37–39.

John Sullivan. "Liturgical Creativity from Edith Stein," *Teresianum* 49 (1998,1), 165–85.

____. "Edith Stein Challenges Catholics," *Teresianum* 50 (1999, 1–2), 335–57.